JUL   2003

LICENSE PLATE BOOK

BY
LEONARD WISE

FIREFLY BOOKS

A FIREFLY BOOK

Published by Firefly Books Ltd., 2002

First Printing

National Library of Canada Cataloguing in Publication Data
Wise, Leonard
          The way cool license plate book / Leonard Wise.

ISBN 1-55297-686-6 (bound).—ISBN 1-55297-563-0 (pbk.)

          1. Games for travelers—Juvenile literature. I. Title.

GV1206.W58 2002   j793.7   C2002-902844-2

Publisher Cataloging-in-Publication Data (U.S.)
Wise, Leonard.
   The way cool license plate book / Leonard Wise.—1st ed.
[64] p. : col. ill. ;   cm.
Summary: Over 350 vanity license plates organized in six categories with jokes, games and activities.
ISBN 1-55297-686-6
ISBN 1-55297-563-0 (pbk.)
1. Automobile license plates—United States—Juvenile literature. I. Title.
388.3/ 422   21   CIP   HE5620.L5.W57 2002

Published in Canada in 2002 by
Firefly Books Ltd.
3680 Victoria Park Avenue
Toronto, Ontario M2H 3K1

Published in the United States in 2002 by
Firefly Books (U.S.) Inc.
P.O. Box 1338, Ellicott Station
Buffalo, New York 14205

Designed by George Walker

License plate illustrations by
Christine Gilham & George Walker

Printed and bound in Canada by
Friesens
Altona, Manitoba

The Publisher acknowledges the financial support of the Government of Canada through the Book Publishing Industry Development Program for its publishing activities.

CONTENTS

INTRODUCTION

MOST PEOPLE know that the word *vain* means to be conceited. The word *vanity* means being vain—having too much pride in your appearance. These days, that word is connected not just to people. A personalized license plate—the kind that people pay extra money for—is called a "vanity plate."

Next time you're out for a drive or walking through a parking lot, check out the vehicles around you. Many of them have vanity plates. While most people still settle for ordinary, everyday plates, there are lots of folks who like to get personal with their cars.

For many people, a vanity plate is an extension of their personality. Quieter types may have a plate that shows only their name, nickname or initials. People who are less shy could have plates that express their love for their car, profession, partner, pet or favorite hobby or sport. A vanity plate can show a person's playful side, mood or favorite saying, or it may be a friendly greeting. Outspoken types prefer to say something funny, trendy or cool, or to use their plates as a chance to brag.

Then again, there are some people who put on messages that are just plain crazy.

For example, on one VW Beetle, the plate said BOBS MG. When someone commented to the owner that the car wasn't an MG, the man replied, "I'm not Bob." Go figure!

The possibilities are limited only by a person's imagination and creativity. By dropping vowels or consonants, and using numbers in place of whole words or parts of them, people can get their point across with very few letters. For example, 2L8 2W8 = too late to wait. And 4U2NV = for you to envy. Get the idea? You can put most words on a plate, as long as you follow the government's rules.

The pages of this book are filled with a fun and fascinating look at some of the endless possibilities for vanity plates. Have a good time decoding them. But this isn't just a book of license plate pictures. There's also a brief history of the use of license plates—plus lots of way cool facts.

Need something to do on your next long car trip? Try out the great license plate games in this book. You'll be at your destination before you have a chance to ask, "Are we there yet?"

There are hours and hours of entertainment in *The Way Cool License Plate Book*. JST4U. HVFUN.

HISTORY

THE LICENSE PLATE as we know it had simple beginnings. In 1901, it was nothing more than the owner's initials painted on the back of the vehicle. Since those initials were too hard for police-men to find and to read, they made a new law. For a $1.00 fee, each vehicle was assigned a registration number. An owner then made his or her own license on a leather pad or metal plate and bolted brass numbers to it. In some states, people made plates out of wood or rubber, or had them made at the local saddlery or blacksmith shop. In Canada, most people made plates out of leather or rubber, and in some cases they paint-ed the numbers right on the car.

In 1903, Massachusetts became the first place to issue state-made license plates. It was a metal plate. Other states soon fol-lowed, with plates made of metal, leather, sheet metal or wooden shingles. At that time, prisoners began to make the license plates. That practice continues today in most states and provinces.

The first vanity plates were offered in Connecticut, in 1937. Other states began offering vanities once they realized how much money could be made. However, some of those plates caused embarrassing problems when the licensing offices couldn't figure out a code. They soon hired special staff to carefully check all plate requests. These days, there are more vanities than ever, and new problems as well. It's also becoming common for thieves to steal the most creative plates.

Did you know there are thousands of people all over the world who collect license plates? Since Internet use has become more commonplace, collectors now have the opportunity to find license plates they used to dream about locating. Collectors can trade with and buy from like-minded people from all over the world. Many collectors stick to a specific theme, such as plates from their birth year, or from every state or province in their country. Some collectors look for motorcycle or farm vehicle plates. Some aim to collect a plate from every country or island in the world. Many col-lectors display their plates on the Internet, both to show off their collec-tion and in the hopes of finding someone to trade with.

Collecting actual license plates isn't the only hobby for plate enthusiasts. Some people just take pictures of the plates they like and make an album or website with them. This practice takes up a lot less room. It's also less costly and a whole lot lighter!

Another very popular hobby is collecting lists of vanity plates. These collectors never leave home without a paper and pencil. They constantly scan traffic and parking lots for new additions. When they see a vanity, they quickly copy it down along with the make and color of the car it's on. They then crack the code and add the plate to their collection list. This hobby is free for anyone who's interested. All you need are paper, pencil and quick reflexes. Happy hunting!

GAMES

Here are a bunch of games you can play when you're on a car trip. They're lots of fun and can really help pass the time. You'll need a pencil or pen, colored pencils, and a pad of paper or a notebook. Have fun!

GAMES FOR YOUNGER KIDS

Rainbow Bingo – This game is for little ones who are too young to read. On a piece of paper, use colored pencils or crayons to make a small circle in each color of the rainbow. You will need red, yellow, orange, green, blue and purple. Try to find all of those colors on the license plates you see. Use a different color to mark an X through each color as you find it. When you've found them all, call out BINGO! You can also use the license plate stickers to find the colors you're looking for.

Alphabet Hunt – On a piece of paper, write down the letters of the alphabet. Look at the letters on license plates and cross out each letter as you see it. Can you find them all?

Color Challenge – For a challenge, try to find as many different-colored license plate stickers as you can. The sticker is found in one corner of the license plate. On a piece of paper, draw small circles using all the colors in your colored pencil case or crayon box. Watch the license plate stickers and mark an X through each color as you find it. See if you can find them all!

EZ Bingo – Write the letters B-I-N-G-O on your paper. Watch the license plates and look for those letters. When you find a letter you're looking for, put an X through it. The first person who finds them all calls out BINGO!

Picture This – See how many license plates you can spot that have pictures or symbols on them. Try to identify the pictures or symbols. Ask for help if you don't recognize something.

A BIT MORE CHALLENGING

Alphabet Safari – On a piece of paper, write down all the letters of the alphabet. Your challenge is to find them in the right order by looking at license plates. Cross them off as you find them. No skipping letters!

Alphabet Zoo – Look at the letters on a license plate, pick a letter, and try to name an animal that starts with that letter. Write down the names. See how many different kinds of animals wind up in your zoo.

Double or Nothing – Try to find license plates that have double numbers or letters – two As, two 3s, two Ds, etc. They don't have to be next to each other. Keep track of the ones you find. See which letter or number gives you the most twins. For a challenge, try to find all the double numbers from 00 to 99 in order. No skipping numbers!

Triple Play – Try to find license plates that have three numbers or letters alike. Follow the same rules as in Double or Nothing – but this time, you're looking for triplets.

Four-Leaf Clover – Rarest of all! Try to find a license plate with four matching numbers or letters. If you're really lucky, you might find more than one!

Flora and Fauna (Plants and Animals) – Look for license plates with pictures of plants or animals on them. Write down where the plate is from, along with the name of the plant or animal. If you can't identify something, you can check it out when you get home. Just look for information on that state, province or country.

Word Search – See how many license plates you can find that have actual words in them. For example, AFRY = a fry; or WEDO = we do. Some plates will contain just one small word. ZHAM = ham. TMEK = me. Write down the word or words you find and see how many you can get.

Initial It – Try to find one license plate that has all of your initials on it. Want an even bigger challenge? Try to find them in the right order! You can also play this game using the initials of each person in your family.

Decoder – Write down the letters and numbers from several vanity plates. Try to figure out what each message says, and write it down next to the "code." See how many plates you can decipher. Some may have more than one possibility.

GAMES

Vanity Plate Creator – Make up some of your own personalized vanity plates using up to eight letters. Here are some ideas: something you like to do; what you'd like to be when you grow up; jobs people do; your favorite animal, sport, team or food; or an expression or saying that you hear or use. Remember, you can make it easier by dropping vowels or consonants, and by using numbers in place of whole words or parts of them.

Team Spirit – See how many license plates you can find that refer to the names of sports teams, team members or sports-related words. Write down the plate names. Group together any plates that relate to the same team. That will show you how popular it is.

Where Are You From? – See how many license plates are from other states, provinces or countries. Write down where they are from and keep a tally of how many you see from each place. When you get home, you can check an atlas or map to see which plate came from the farthest away.

Friends and Neighbors – Pick a person who you know and write his or her first name on your paper. Watch the license plates and try to find all the letters of that name in the correct order. (You may need several plates to find all the letters.) Cross off each letter as you go. When you're done, pick another name.

Famous Players – Write down the name of a TV or movie star, your favorite character from a show or movie, or the name of a movie that you've seen. Watch the license plates and try to find all the letters from that name. Cross off each letter as you find it. If you want more of a challenge, try to find the letters in the right order.

Funny Phrases and Words – Write down the letters from any license plate and try to make up funny phrases or words using the letters in the order you see them. Here are some examples: FHOP = Frogs Hate Old Pickles, SPHM = Silly Purple-Haired Monkeys, AKLT = A Kilt or A Kangaroo Licking Tomatoes, and YPEK = Yuck! Pink Elephant Kisses. Have fun!

Year-Long Bingo – The sticker on a license plate gives an abbreviation of the month the license expires. Write the following on your paper: Jan, Feb, Mar, Apr, May, Jun, Jul, Aug, Sep, Oct, Nov, Dec. Since some areas use numbers instead of letters, you should also number each month from 1 to 12. Put an X through each month as you find it. The first person who finds all 12 months calls out BINGO! For a bigger challenge, try to find the months in the right order.

Toy Box – Look at a license plate and pick a letter from it. Write the letter on your paper and try to think of the name of a well-known toy that begins with that letter. For example, B = Barbie, S = Slinky, K = Kermit the Frog. Write down the name of the toy, then see how many different toys are in your toy box by the end of the game.

GAMES

NOW FOR A REAL CHALLENGE

Bingo Challenge – Each person writes on the top of their paper all the letters of the alphabet and the numbers from 0 to 9. Below this list, players make a grid five columns wide and five rows long. This is the bingo card. Each player now randomly chooses a combination of letters and numbers to put into the grid. It's best if the letters and numbers are not in order. (Cross them off the list as they're used.) Next, someone chooses a license plate for everyone to copy down. Each player now looks at his or her card and circles those letters and numbers that appear on the license plate. Continue choosing license plates and circling letters and numbers on the card. The first person to complete any vertical, horizontal or diagonal line calls BINGO!

Switching Places – On vanity plates, numbers and letters are often used to take the place of whole words or parts of them. For example, W8 = wait, 4 = for, U = you, C = see, R = are or our, sox = socks. Watch for letters and numbers that have switched places, and write them down with their meanings beside them. See how many you can find.

Anagrams – On a piece of paper, write down the letters from any license plate. (It helps to have at least one vowel.) Rearrange the letters and write down any words that you make from them. Example: From TREA you can get *tea, tear, rate, at* and *eat.* Do you see any others?

Seasonal Bingo – Write on your paper the months of each season, separated into four seasonal groups: For Winter, use Jan, Feb, Mar. For Spring, use Apr, May, Jun. Summer is Jul, Aug, Sep. And Fall is Oct, Nov, Dec. You should also number each month from 1 to 12. Be sure to number them correctly! Watch the license plate stickers and mark off each month as you see it. The first person to mark off all three in any one season calls BINGO!

Making connections – Some vanity plate messages may seem a little odd or make no sense to you. Try to make a connection between the plate and the car that it's on. Examples: IML8 on a white Volkswagen Rabbit *(Alice in Wonderland)*; SSSNAKE on a Cobra or a Viper. Be a super sleuth and keep track of how many connections you make.

OCCUPATIONS

PLATE FACTS

Wyoming's cowboy and bucking bronco have appeared on its plates since 1936, making it the oldest license plate design in continuous use.

I FIX-BAX - Sore backs really hurt. Take care of yours, or see this doctor.

SA AH - If you do this, we'll be able to see right down your throat.

AV 8R - Anyone who flies a plane could use this plate.

BOWK4U - If you like flowers, I can make a bouquet for you.

FLY GUY - This guy wants you to know he loves to fly a plane.

TRUCKIT - Driving big trucks is a tough job.

HIZZONR - When you talk about a mayor or judge, you say "his honor."

12

K9 TUTR - A tutor is a special teacher. This one has gone to the dogs.

FIRE - Idaho faces dangerous forest fires every summer.

BUGKLR - Call the exterminator if you've got bugs.

ISU4U - I'm a lawyer who fights for you in court.

RNOV8R - Don't move—this fellow will fix up your house just as good as new.

IDOHAIR - Come to me when it's just too long to manage.

PIPE DR- Plumbing problems? I'm your man.

PLATE FACTS

The world's oldest license plate slogan is Vacationland, first used in Maine in 1935.

OCCUPATIONS

4CASTR - I can tell you everything about tomorrow's weather.

FATNOMO - I'll teach you how to eat and exercise to keep that fat off.

TIMBR - Only by planting more trees will we have something to cut in the future.

W8 TR - The man to see when you're really hungry.

MAKMLAF - Make them laugh. That's what comedians do—funny guy.

9WUNWUN - Emergency! Dial 911 for police and fire.

REALST8 - Houses, farms and buildings—that's all real estate.

TV NUS - Every night, television shows you what happened around the world.

DEEP 6 - Throw it overboard and I'll go get it.

PLATE FACTS

The rarest American plates are the 1921 Alaska and the 1912 Mississippi.

C GOOD - Visit your eye doctor twice a year and you will!

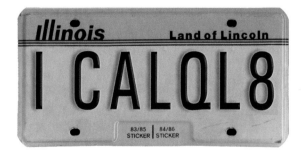

I CALQL8 - I can do math really fast with my little calculator.

15

OCCUPATIONS

DAFUZZ - Maybe some police have a sense of humor.

EDUC8R - The adult at the front of the classroom!

HITEC - Computers and the Internet are all very high tech.

DJ - Spin those records and we'll dance.

FAB CAB - Nice Taxi! Does it cost more to ride in your car?

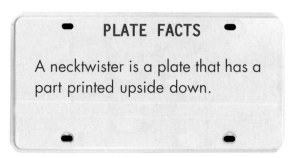

PLATE FACTS

A necktwister is a plate that has a part printed upside down.

2 DRESU - My job is to make sure you look very nice.

SHO4 - I'll drive you anywhere you want to go.

RETIRED - Now that I don't have to go to work, I'm not tired at all.

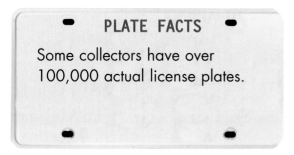

PLATE FACTS

Some collectors have over 100,000 actual license plates.

PAID2RGU - Lawyers are paid to argue for you in court.

DOC LAW - Don't argue with this guy —he's a legal professor.

DOC 4 JOX - Special sports medicine doctors take care of professional athletes.

XCAV8R - If you need a big hole, just call me.

K9 DR - Sick dogs are my specialty —I'll make them well fast.

COP 2B - Before they graduate, all police are this.

OCCUPATIONS

2020 - See me when you need glasses.

TICKDOC - Sometimes your heart is called a "ticker." This doctor will keep it healthy.

PPR BOY - I'll be by to collect on Friday.

SPUDS 4U - This guy grows lots of potatoes.

PLATE FACTS

Fiberboard and a pressed soybean and paper mixture were used during war times to conserve metal.

SAYCHEEZ - I can get anybody to smile for my camera.

KARTUNS - I write and draw cartoons for the newspaper.

FONFIXER - I work for the phone company. Give me a call.

HUDUNIT - I don't know. Let's hope the police can figure it out.

LECHEF - French cooks serve great food.

DZYNR - A good designer makes anything look better.

ZOOMAN - I love working with animals. The zoo is perfect for me.

BUG MUGR - I can rid your home of insects in just a few hours!

DRYANKM - Take care of your teeth or you'll need to visit me.

KEY MAN - Locked out? Call the locksmith and get new keys made.

PLATE FACTS

In 1942, Delaware became the last state to issue a porcelain plate.

OCCUPATIONS

PLATE FACTS

The 1941 Georgia plate was the first reflectorized general issue plate in the US. It was also the first plate to use a decal.

FIZIKAL - Not everything is mental. Sometimes you need to use your body, too.

CRE8IV - I'm an artist, so I'm naturally creative.

ANIM8R - My drawings make the movies that kids love best.

SO ITUP - Make your own clothes, and you'll always have something to wear.

IDIGIT - Get your shovel and head for the garden.

2THDR - Teeth hurt? See your dentist.

IDELVR - Deliver what? Pizza? Babies? Packages?

MAXIMUM 30

MEGABYT - I'm into computers in a big way.

PIZZAMN - Make mine a large cheese and pepperoni, please.

PLATE FACTS

In 1956, all states began making license plates the same size.

ADMUP - Do your math homework carefully, and you'll get the right answer.

SHUTRBUG - Take your camera wherever you go.

IM4 TAX - This guy must work for the government.

OCCUPATIONS

PLATE FACTS

During WWII, some states used a soy-bean-based fiberboard to make license plates. Goats really liked them—to eat!

MDRN - We'll be fine. The doctor and the nurse are in this car.

TAXIMUM - This mother spends lots of time driving the kids around.

RUNSRNS - Do you have any errands to run? This guy can do them.

BRD FANCR - Lots of people love our little feathered friends.

SOOPER - This driver manages an apartment building.

I FOTOU - Smile and say cheese when you see my camera.

NODK4U - This plate belongs to a dentist. Did you floss today?

2 REPOU - This guy works for the finance company.

LDY TEC - She's a lady auto technician.

P8NTR - I wonder if they paint houses or pictures of houses.

IDEZYNE - She must be a designer.

PLATE FACTS

To conserve metal during WWI, plates in Ontario were made of stiff cardboard in 1915 and 1916.

ANIMALS

PLATE FACTS

In 1903, Massachusetts issued its first plate to Frederick Tudor. That plate is still held as an active registration by his family, almost 100 years later.

BOW WOW - Arf Arf.

BIZZEB - I'm black and yellow and very busy.

JARAF - My neck is longer than my legs!

BRDDOG - I can't fly, but I'm a real pointer.

BUMBLB - I'm hard at work making honey.

SSSNAKE - Just watch me sssslither.

GIDIUP - Stop horsing around and get going.

C1GECKO - Seen one, seen 'em all.

2NAFISH - If you can do that, you must be able to tune a guitar.

KLRSHEEP - This shepherd has the best sheep in all of Montana.

OINK - I may sound funny, but everyone loves my curly tail.

9LIVES - Even with 9 lives, I always watch for cars.

MEOW - I'm a cool cat.

ANIMALS

WART HOG - Wart hogs can run fast and are very courageous.

WYLDLYF - Parties in the wilderness are my thing.

K9 PALZ - Dogs are my best friends.

POOCH - I love my dog best.

MS PIGGY - I'm in love with a frog!

GR8 BEAR - The bigger the bear, the faster I run.

FRE BRD - I'm free as a bird!

EEGL - Sometimes I'm bald, but I can always fly.

BIGDAWG - Big dog, big bite.

KTTN - A mother cat can have several of these.

HUFBEAT - Toe-tapping music for animals.

HOOT - A wise old bird makes this sound.

Elk Ahead/crossing sign, Arizona

ANIMALS

WOLFMAN - Don't get near me during a full moon.

BIGBIRD - Lives on Sesame Street.

KINGFISH - Everybody else in the ocean takes orders from me.

KOOGR - I'm just like a mountain lion.

SHARKY - I'd love to take a bite out of you next time you're swimming.

SCRATCH - Only when you're itchy and never on the furniture.

MUTT - Definitely not a purebred.

CATLUVR - Only the best is good enough for my pet.

28

LEFANT - I'm the largest animal in Africa.

SKEETR - Summer nights are my favorite time to feed.

CRABBY - My legs taste especially good.

FLUTRBY - Butterflies do this if you see them in the garden.

PLATE FACTS

Virginia is the only state that issued embossed fiberboard plates.

WING22 - There are 11 birds here.

ANIMALS

I SPYDER - One is enough for most people.

HOW LIN - This will send shivers up your spine.

POSSUM - I can hang by my tail and play dead, too.

H2O K9 - This mutt just loves to swim.

CAT NAP - Not while you're driving, I hope?

BIG 2TH - I have a dinosaur tooth from the Badlands.

GR 8DANE - A really, really big dog.

O DEAR - Oh Deer? What could the matter be?

ARF ARF - It's OK, boy! It's only a turtle.

BIG BUX - This plate belongs on a very expensive car.

BROWNCOW - How now, friend?

UNICORN - Mythical beasts are what I like.

ROAR - Lions love to open wide and…

TYGR - I love the orange because it matches my stripes.

31

MY JEEP - But maybe someday you can have one of your own.

4ONDFLOR - This car is not automatic —I've got to do the work.

SLANT6 - This old engine really moves.

MYVET - America's ultimate sports car is all mine.

KLUNCAR - Some days I'm surprised I can get it to go.

MYWHLS - All five of them are mine.

LORIDR - Riding close to the road.

THEJAG - Not the animal in the forest.

HUMMR - Arnold has one…and I do, too.

REBILT - Waste not, want not.

MUSSLCR - Big fat engine with power to spare.

FLORIT - Put the pedal to the metal.

TUF CAR - This car was built to last.

FASTNUF - But not too fast.

AHEDAU - If you can read this you're behind me.

FASTRNU - But we get to the light together!

CAR TERMS

MY BEETL - I love my bug.

WABBIT - Oh, you wascal.

CADDY - This baby takes me everywhere in style.

MINIVAN - I may be mini, but I'm no mouse!

BEEMER - This little car is from Bavaria.

BIG BUG - Too big to step on.

EAT DUST - Nobody gets ahead of me!

PLATE FACTS

Palindromes are plates that are the same read forward and backward. 10AXA01 is a perfect palindrome.

VET NUT - I love my stingray best.

MY TOY - This Toyota is just for me.

ZOOOM - That's all you'll hear as I go by.

DEUCE - Deuces have only two doors.

IMBLIND - Let's hope this driver is just joking.

FILRUP - This car will pass everything but a gas station.

CAR TERMS

BYBY2U - See you later.

4KIX - This car is just for fun.

2 AWSUM - There is nothing more I can say to praise this car.

SUN BUG - My VW has a sun roof.

PLATE FACTS

In 1928, after suffering one of the worst years in fishing history, Massachusetts fishermen blamed their license plate. It showed a fish swimming away from the word Massachusetts.

DNTB2NR - Keep back a safe distance in case I have to stop.

CYCOCAR - That's one crazy car!

ON TYME - Surprise! Somebody is actually on time.

BBEEP - What the Road Runner says.

4RD TRK - Built Ford Tough.

IM L8 - Would look especially good on a white VW Rabbit.

MOV OVR - Please get your car out of my way.

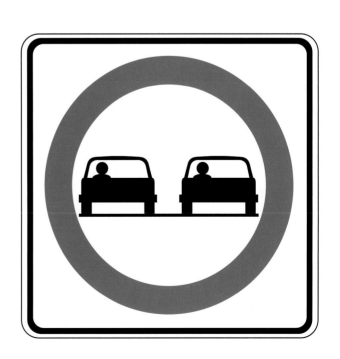

CAR TERMS

PLATE FACTS

From 1907 to 1917, Texas vehicles were registered by individual counties. Since there were over 200 counties, that meant over 200 cars might have the same license number.

LEMMING - I don't know where I'm going—I just follow everyone else.

SCREECH - That's the sound of my tires as I come to a sudden stop!

OIMSOL8 - No matter what I try, I just feel further behind.

GUZZLER - This car uses gas like fish use water.

T BIRD - Nice bird...I mean car!

EXCLAMATIONS

AINTME - So who is it then?

ADIOS - So long for now.

ATTABOY - Way to go, my boy.

IW84NO1 - I'm always in a hurry.

GR8EST - That about explains how I feel about my car.

CHILOUT - But don't get too frosty.

UREKA - What a great discovery!

NOPROB - Then it must be easy.

EXCLAMATIONS

OUCH - I need a bandage.

PITZ - This car is no good at all.

SWEET - Am I sweet enough for you?

IAMYY4U - I'm just too "y's" for you!

QTPI - Pretty good looking car, too.

ACHOO - Gesundheit!

GRRR8 - Tony the Tiger says…

STR8AS - I got top marks in all my classes at school.

EXCLAMATIONS

WOWWOW - Very impressive!

IMAQT - Everybody says I look nice.

OOOPS - ... I did it again!

NEAT - I hate a mess.

4SHUR - There is no doubt about it, I'm sure.

WAT EVR - Whatever you want is fine with me.

OOLALA - This little French car is a beauty.

CYAH - See you later.

EXCLAMATIONS

WATS 2C - There's lots to see, just look around you.

HUMMIN - Very small birds.

A10SHN - Pay attention men, I've got something to say.

OKYDOKY - OK, I agree with you.

HAHA - There is no gold in that pan.

COWPIE - Don't step on me.

TRRIFK - Things couldn't be better.

2M8OS - Used to make ketchup.

EXCLAMATIONS

IV ADIT - You've had it? What have you had?

LOCO - Just plumb crazy.

JIVIN - Jitterbug and boogie.

COMIK - Very funny fellows who make you laugh.

FREQOUT - Whenever I see a snake.

FNOMNL - Just astounding.

R WE THER - How much further?

YEP YEP - Sorry, I don't agree. Nope, nope.

EXCLAMATIONS

KLUTZ - I tend to drop things.

OMAN - Oh boy!

HIS - Certainly not hers.

VLI KEU - They like me! They really like me!

ZOOM - Zoom, Zoom and you'll get there quicker.

YOOOO - This plate will get my attention!

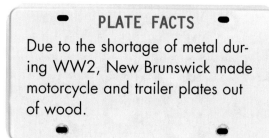

PLATE FACTS

Due to the shortage of metal during WW2, New Brunswick made motorcycle and trailer plates out of wood.

FLYIN - Watch this guy, he drives too fast. He thinks he's a bird.

BOSOX - My red socks tell you I play for Boston.

OVERBAR - Pick up your feet and you'll clear it nicely.

ASTROS - I'm from Houston. There's no baseball in space.

KNICKS - Pro basketball is big in New York.

BEARS - Some people are surprised to find bears in Chicago.

JOGR - I only use the car for long trips. I'd rather be running.

1STBASE - Some days I just can't seem to get there.

SPORTS TERMS

BUCKIS - Ohio basketball.

JAYS - Toronto baseball.

COACH - He's the boss.

YANKEES - New York baseball.

GIANC - Big fans of football.

CELTICS - Boston basketball.

RANGER - Everything is big in Texas.

BICEPS - Big muscles, but what about the car?

HABS - Montreal Canadiens hockey, eh?

GOALI - Puck stopper.

OILERS - Edmonton hockey.

RDWINGZ - Detroit hockey.

KINGS - Los Angeles hockey.

BRUINS - Boston hockey.

STARS - Can be found in the heavens and on the ice.

LEAFS - Toronto hockey. Go Leafs Go!

SPORTS TERMS

SLALOM - It's all downhill from here.

14 HORSE - We can make a race out of this.

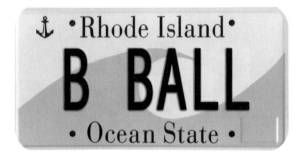

B BALL - Played with a basket.

TMBRWOLF - B-ball with the Minnesota Timberwolves is all right.

W8LIFTR - Clean and jerk wins the prize.

GATOR - Not to be confused with a crocodile.

BALANCE - Try and keep yours at all times.

MOGUL - Skiing the bumps.

12 PIPE - Half a tube is better than none.

HAT TRIC - Three goals and it's a Hat Trick.

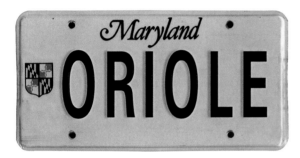

ORIOLE - Flying in from Baltimore.

4WRD PAS - The fastest way to a first down.

3 POINTS - How much do you need to win?

SCORES - Keep track of yours and we'll see who wins.

CHMPYNS - We are the champions of the world.

HOMER - Hit one with the bases loaded.

SPORTS TERMS

BLITZ - Sack the quarterback.

DEFENSE - Nothing too offensive.

REELMEN - We like fishing best.

KUNG FU - Everybody was fighting.

HOL N1 - Every golfer's dream.

H2OSKR - You'll find me at the end of a rope behind my boat.

DEKE IT - Fake it, deke it, just get around it.

SAILZ - I love my boat on a windy day.

SPORTS TERMS

STRIKE - You only get three of these and you're out.

UROUT - That third strike must have just caught the corner.

SLAM - Basketball power shot.

PITCHIT - And I'll catch it.

SLICE - The opposite of a hook.

TEE ITUP - This driver must love to play golf.

BULRIDR - On the horns of a dilemma.

4MULA1 - One expensive race car.

SAYINGS

PLATE FACTS

In 1918, Florida became the last state to introduce state-wide license plates.

2 EZ - I guess there was no challenge in that.

NOSMOX - It's bad for your health—so don't smoke.

8CHEEZ - I did too, but do you get paid for it?

HEZ MYN - OK he's yours, you can have him.

PUTM UP - Put 'em up, or shut up.

2L8 2W8 - He's just out of time.

CU THAR - We'll see you when you get there.

CANUCME - Because I can see you fine.

U8NT ME - No I guess I'm not, and that sure isn't my car.

H82BL8 - In fact, I always try to be early.

LST 2NO - Are you always the last to find out?

2 DY4 - There is nothing I want more.

EZ AS PI - Even if it is not so easy to make, it sure is easy to eat.

53

SAYINGS

FUN4U - These plates are fun for me, too.

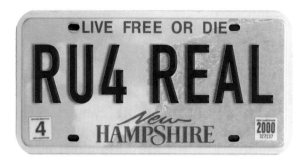

RU4 REAL - Or are you pretending to be someone else?

4U2NV - This car is for me to enjoy and you to envy.

22 TANGO - It only takes two to tango.

IM HERS - She's mine.

ICULAFN - I see you laughing at my car—cut it out!

PSAKAKE - Is that chocolate or vanilla?

SWEE2TH - Soon I'll have to see my dentist.

WAYKOOL - Maybe it's time to turn off the air-conditioning.

LUV U2 - Obviously a very affectionate driver.

RUD14ME - And am I the one for you?

IWUNIT - I won this in a contest. I'm so lucky.

HI 5 - Give me one.

BIMI UP - Do it Scotty.

NITS FUR - I wonder if she knits anything else? NITS WUL perhaps?

SNT KLAS - I've been good. Hope you bring me lots for Christmas.

SAYINGS

EMAJIN - Imagine me in a car like that.

CEN CBL - Now that is one sensible car.

ALEON - Is that Albert Leon? Or are you from another planet?

YTRY - Y try to catch me? You'll never do it.

ICSTARS - I love to use my telescope on dark nights.

COOLIT - Put it in the fridge.

PLATE FACTS

In 1909, the Canadian government issued its own plates made of rubber.

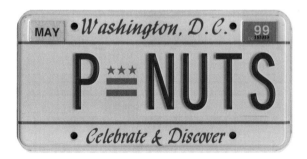

P NUTS - Make sure you don't make a mess with the shells.

PLATE FACTS
On Christmas Eve, 1903, England issued its first automobile license plate.

JES KIDN - You didn't think I was serious, did you?

A OK - Never felt better in my life.

GR8 BOOX - Obviously a book lover.

4ME 2NO - For me to know and you to find out.

SNOMAN - That's why I live in the north.

XPLOSV - Stand back, this guy is dangerous.

BRLYTHR - "Bearly" there! Where's the bear? Are we there yet?

SAYINGS

2S DAY - The day after Monday.

NVRMND - Never you mind either.

CUL8R - Alligator.

IM L8 - You're late? I'm behind you!

EZ4U - I wish it was as easy for me.

ILBCNU - I'll be seeing you too!

GOTCHA - You sure did!

HOBBIT - I'm a real Tolkien fan, are you?

HOPARU - Hop to it.

WHY NOT - I don't know why not!

PHISHIN - That's where you'll find me on weekends.

PLATE FACTS
To reflectorize plates, tiny glass beads were once put on letters and numbers.

RUBRDUKY - But I'll never get this car in the tub.

DN THAT - Been there too.

KWILTZ - Stitching and sewing are my hobbies.

XLNT - Very good indeed.

SAYINGS

14GET - Absent-minded driver.

W8 4U - Wait for you—but not for long.

GO4IT - Might as well try.

24KT - Pure gold from the Klondike, home of the gold rush.

KPASA - Whatever will be, will be.

EEEEEK - Come on, it wasn't that scary.

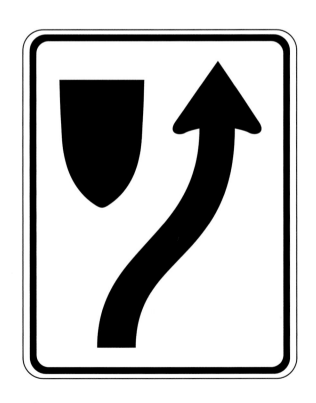

IDIDNT - Don't blame me, I didn't do it either.

T HEEE - Mildly amusing.

Y BCUZ - Just because?

I CAN CU - I can see you too.

2HIP4U - I'm too hip for you too.

XQSME - Well pardon me.

2NRVS - An anxious driver.

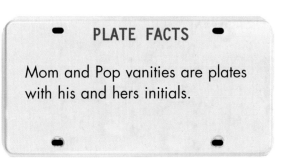

PLATE FACTS

Mom and Pop vanities are plates with his and hers initials.

SAYINGS

HVA BITE - This is a delicious cake. Have a bite.

URTHE1 - You're the one for me.

SPARCL - You certainly have a bright sparkle and shine about you!

YESNDD - Are you a yes man?

YME - Because we've got to blame somebody.

02 BME - Is it nice being you?

MAKMYDY - Go ahead, make my day. I dare you.

CRAZ4U - I'm glad you like me so much.

H82 LIE - Here's an honest person.

2D MALL - A professional shopper.

20LD4U - Find somebody your own age.

ZATSO - Yes, that's so. Want to make something of it.

BADMUDE - Being stuck in traffic puts me in a bad mood.

4MY BRO - It's nice to see some brotherly love.

BCNYA - Not if I see you first.

PLATE FACTS

During WWII, Quebec made license plates out of Masonite.

EXPLORE CANADA'S ARCTIC
THE END
NORTHWEST TERRITORIES

FLORIDA
MONTH • YEAR
ADEOS
Protect Wild Dolphins

HAWAII
ITS OVR
ALOHA STATE

19 Georgia 90
NO MO

West Virginia
BYE
Wild, Wonderful

•Massachusetts• YEAR
THANK U
•The Spirit of America•

BON VOYAGE!